20 Ways

to Lose Your **Lover**

(20 Ways to Keep Your Lover)

Stephanie Goldman Meis, MA, LCPC

BALBOA.PRESS
A DIVISION OF HAY HOUSE

Balboa Press books may be ordered through booksellers or by contacting:

Balboa Press
A Division of Hay House
1663 Liberty Drive
Bloomington, IN 47403
www.balboapress.com
844-682-1282

Print information available on the last page.

ISBN: 979-8-7652-3809-7 (sc)
ISBN: 979-8-7652-3808-0 (hc)
ISBN: 979-8-7652-3807-3 (e)

Library of Congress Control Number: 2023900988

Balboa Press rev. date: 11/08/2023

BACKGROUND

The author, Stephanie Meis, MA LCPC, Reiki Master Teacher is a psychotherapist in Highland Park, Illinois where she helps and supports others who are open to spirituality as well as psychotherapy. She is happily married (with a reasonable amount of problems) to her second husband and has two grown children and one growing granddaughter. The information in this book is a concentrated form of Stephanie's life-long collection of wisdom to understand how and why humans have such a hard time in relationships. Stephanie's collection of information comes from 2 marriages, 15 years of spiritual study –Jewish Mysticism, 7 years in Energy Healing School, 25 years studying and using the Internal Family Systems, 45 years teaching and playing violin professionally in Chicago and 20 years as a Reiki Master Teacher and psychotherapist. Her purpose in writing this book is to offer you, the reader, a simple and straight-forward way to have better relationships for a better life!

INTRO

20 WAYS TO LOSE YOUR LOVER

Relationships that don't work are like a cancer.

Cancer is where destructive cells take over healthy cells that may be weakened or stressed in some way. Ideally, our relationships are opportunities for us to get together with others and share love (in the form of support, caring, understanding, fun, the pleasure of sex, kids, nature, food or the world). We also can use these relationships to work through unfinished traumas, pain or wounding from earlier times in our lives.

Usually both opportunities are present.

It's easy to confuse the two. We usually come together because it's wonderful! After a while it gets safe to be with this person and our unfinished stuff automatically comes up to be resolved. The confusing part is like cancer. When our pain comes up, it starts to lower our frequencies and we are not in a good place. This is accompanied by the cancer of blame, fear, passivity, despair and anger and distracting behaviors such as addiction and cheating. These can take over the health of our wonderful feelings for our partner. This is a book about learning to own your own feelings, and become aware of the symptomatic habits of the emotional cancer that can take over when your old stuff is up for resolution.

And yes, old stuff can be resolved!

ACKNOWLEDGEMENTS

This book came from a well-spring of life learning. My husband, children and granddaughter keep me on my toes, learning and growing. Their reading and guidance in creating this book has been invaluable. I am blessed with very wise friends and colleagues: Dina Kaplan, Amy Shimoni, and Linda Zimmerman who edited, discussed and supported this project.

Working with Artist Cheryl Steigler has been pure joy! It is a pleasure to see how she captures Emotion and humor in her wonderful drawings.

I am indebted to Balboa Press and Ann Minoza for turning this idea into a printed book that I hope will help others to understand and improve their close relationships.

20 Ways

to Lose Your **Lover**

1

If you want to lose your lover don't learn about boundaries, meaning "what's mine, what's hers?" This refers to Time, Money, Space, Personal style, Body, Physical touch, Language, Principles, Friends, Car, Projects, Health, Pets, Children, etc.

2

Don't ask for what you want and need. Don't spend time learning what you really want or need.

3

Assume that you know what she/he or others are thinking or feeling.

4

Don't look for negative patterns that have been in your life since before you met him/ her. Patterns that need awareness and change. Don't seek help to work through these things. Tell yourself that change is impossible or not worth the effort.

5

Overcrowd your schedule so there will never be relaxed time to be spontaneously loving and present together.

6

Talk about your EX a lot.

7

Compare your partner to others in the neighborhood, at work and people you previously dated. Make sure she/he comes out hopelessly looking worse than everyone else.

8

Don't be generous. (with money, treating friends, family, gifts, time, walking her/his dog, buying cat food, changing the litter box, getting groceries, picking up dirty clothes or tissues.) If you see that your partner has left the lights on, don't turn them off. Use it as an opportunity to correct her/him.

9

Don't make plans or set aside time to honor nice events such as birthdays, celebrations, and travel.

10

Don't take responsibility for your own feelings. BLAME him/her when things go wrong.

11

Don't stay in the present. Bring up old painful subjects again and again, long after they have been resolved, and describe how negative the future will be.

12

Don't tell your partner when you really like something he's doing, or when you really feel love for her.

13

Don't learn the specifics of your partner's sexual anatomy and exactly how to touch and where he/she likes to be touched. Don't look online for new information about making love, old information (like the Kama Sutra) from other cultures who discovered ways to give pleasure, and don't ask your partner (not in bed) if she/he is happy with your sex life.

14

Think negative thoughts about your partner for hours a day. It will bring your vibration down and he/she will feel it as well, even if he/she can't put his/her finger on why it feels bad.

15

Don't forgive. Don't let go of negative feelings.

16

Don't learn about forgiveness by reading in the other half of this book "The Laws of Teshuvah" or returning to our wholeness after hurting or being hurt by your partner.

17

Exaggerate and dramatize your negative reactions and melt-downs. Feel that you are justified in making your partner distressed by your out-of-control explosions. Hold onto the trauma you've had in your life as a ticket to be unhappy and make your partner pay for how you were cheated in life. Never tell your partner in a light-hearted, humorous or calm way what is really bothering you.

18

Freeze out your partner by staying silent for hours or days when you are upset. Enjoy punishing her/him.

19

Forget about going inside to calm, love and nurture your own inner child when you are upset. Leave yourself feeling bad and blame your partner for your self-neglect. Scare your inner child by focusing on the worst-case scenarios and possible negative future outcomes.

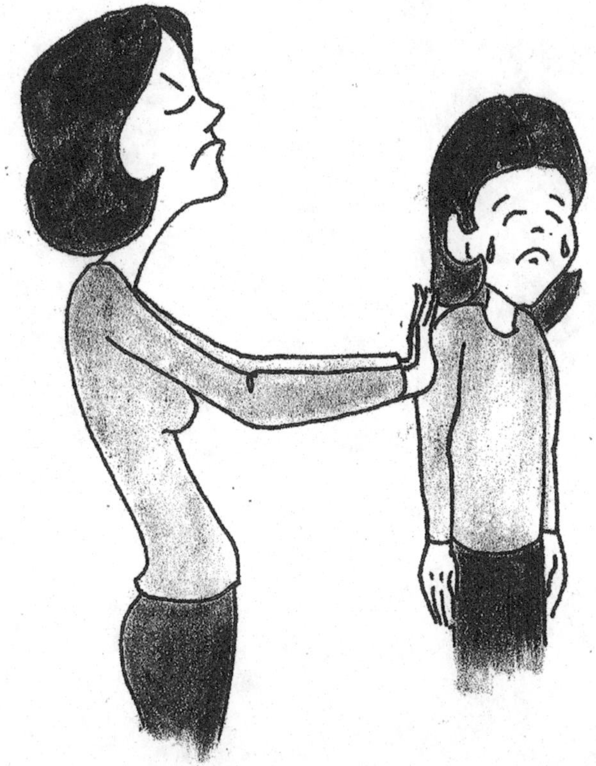

20

Don't speak up for yourself (your inner child) when there is injustice, unkindness, wrong or offense. Assume that you'll never be heard or understood. This will create a feeling of being betrayed. The next step is being angry with yourself and with your partner for not understanding you. This will feel bad!

TURN THIS BOOK UPSIDE DOWN TO LEARN
20 WAYS TO KEEP YOUR LOVER.

20 Ways

to Keep Your **Lover**

1

Be Generous with money, time and praise.

2

Switch from being critical of your partner
to being grateful for her/him.

3

Learn what makes your Lover feel loved and cherished and do these things or say these words. Even a special pet name that she/he chooses can do the trick.

4

Use "I" statements, instead of "You" statements. Say I don't feel comfortable or good when you do or don't do this. And sometimes you'll have a sense it's not a good time to share how you feel.

5

Take ownership for your own inner child. Take excellent care of him/her. This includes listening quietly inside to know what you really want or don't want. Don't wait to eat when you're hungry (even if he/she isn't yet hungry) or wait too long for a bathroom break (even she doesn't want to stop the car). It's easy to feel angry or resentful toward your partner if you don't take care of yourself.

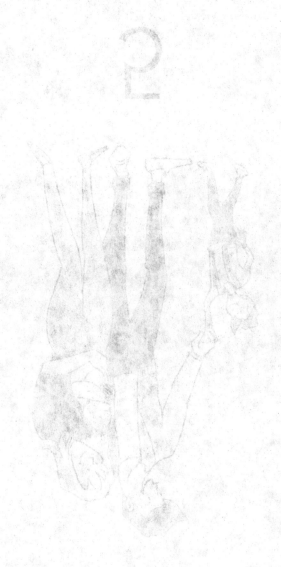

5

Take responsibility for your own inner child: take excellent care of him/her. This includes listening quietly inside to know what you really want or don't want. Don't wait to eat when you're hungry (even if he/she isn't yet hungry) or wait too long for a bathroom break (even she doesn't want to stop the car). It's easy to feel angry or resentful toward your partner if you don't take care of yourself.

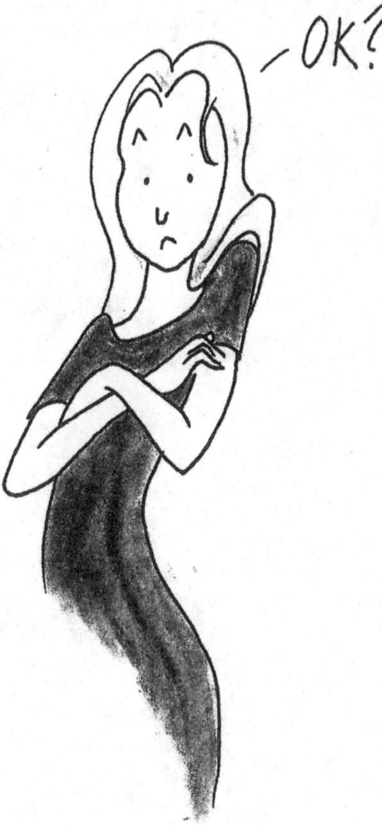

6

Don't ask if your partner wants something after you've decided you want it. For example, when you are in the mood for ice cream, say: "Would you like ice cream?" If she says, "Not really." You've just handed her the final choice and no ice cream for you! Better to say, "I'd like some ice cream. Would you like to join me?" This way you can take good care of your inner child!

7

See your partner as a person from a different culture than yours. She/he may have different ways of expressing emotions, needs, wants. Different ways of thinking or not thinking about things. Trust that these ways of being deserve your love, understanding and patience.

8

No judgment. This is crucial to relationships! Try to notice/perceive/ learn how she/ he is. Say to yourself: "Look at that!" Watch or even tally how many times a day you judge your partner or others. Judgement tends to turn inward later and make you miserable.

9

Remember that it's not your job
to educate or improve him/her.
His/her soul has that responsibility.

10

Tell the truth. No secrets or lies or half-truths. They always feels like betrayal and undermines trust.

11

Be kind. Be kind to yourself and you will find yourself naturally more kind to your partner and others.

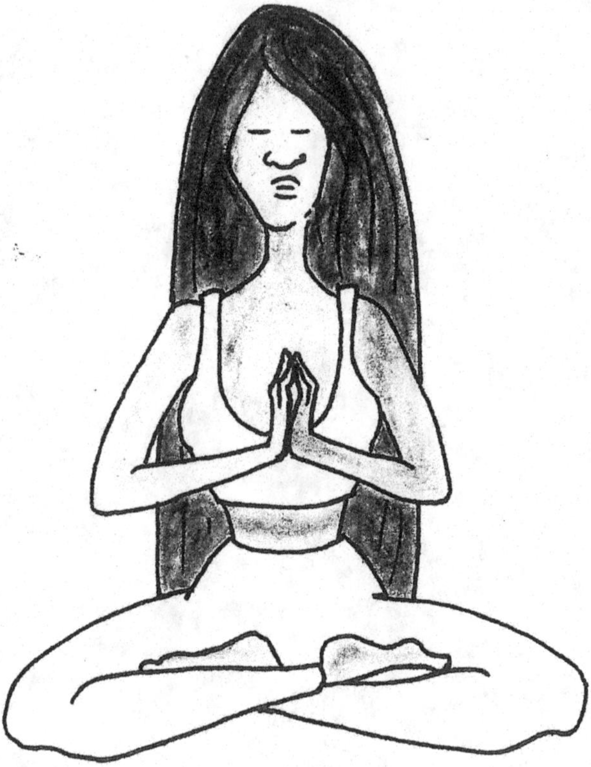

12

Take some time for yourself. When you are very emotional, learn to sit quietly, journal, walk or meditate with your intense feelings to center yourself. Your partner is not responsible to be a container for everything you feel. If you share your negativity about your partner with others, they may tell it back to you in the future when you are already feeling differently.

13

Don't assume. No mind reading allowed. Facts and information are the way to go. They help you to stay away from false conclusions and false reactions (false narratives).

14

Stay in the present as much as you can. Avoid writing the script about the future or rehashing the past which usually hurts.

15

Develop a philosophy about the abundance of the Universe. It will be entirely personal to you. Think about all the ways things come to you that you had nothing to do with. Like: your next breath, your heart beating, a baby being born 9 months after you had sex, the sunrise, the moon, beautiful flowers, good friends, etc.

16

Avoid blame. A good motto is: "It takes two to tango!" Blaming shifts the responsibility to the other person. We are here to learn and evolve and we do this in our everyday interactions.

17

Become knowledgeable about sex. Learn what feels good to your partner and then put some energy into variety: flowers, oils, candles, music, foods, clothing, touch, new techniques.

18

Learn to ask yourself what's more important. For example being available to your partner to share love may have to take priority over folding the laundry or making a phone call. We all have parts that are inner "Managers" who want things under control, but love and happiness come in a free-flowing environment that may not always keep the house perfectly clean or the schedule right on time.

19

Have a regular "date" each week with your lover and honor it. Eating often goes well after sex — so that you can feel light and graceful in bed.

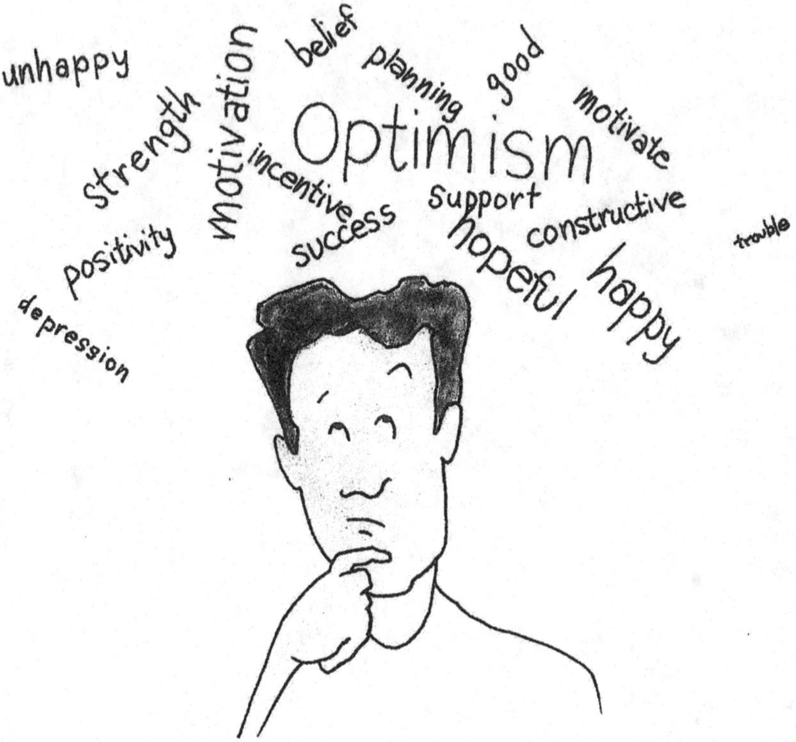

20

Learn to let go of negative thoughts. Be a source of positive energy for yourself and your partner. See these thoughts floating away like helium balloons or puffy clouds or being wiped clean off a dry-erase board. Picture a clear blue sky.

TOOLS

8 Techniques To Help With Your Emotions

BREATH

There is a wonderful, unique phenomenon that can intervene in even the worst of emotional surges:

Your Breath!

Yogis have known this for centuries. Hatha yoga relies upon a smooth flow of relaxed belly breathing to go deeper into the body and release tension to enable a higher state of consciousness.

In 1999 Scientists Doc Childre and Howard Martin published The Heartmath Solution, teaching a way to unite your wandering, sometimes frantic mind with your heart by using a 5 count (5 second) in-sbreath and out-breath! If you're open, try that now for 5 breath cycles. Watch yourself calm down as new soothing chemicals are released by your inner pharmacy. With this breath pattern, your brain will go into an Alpha wave state. I encourage you to check out the Heartmath program (www.Heartmath.com) on your computer or cell phone. It also creates a state of harmony in your body called "congruence" where you align your heart beat with your breath with your Alpha brainwaves. This is the state of deep relaxation I use with my clients to do healing in their subconscious minds.

TONGLEN MEDITATION

Thanks to the Buddhist Monks and Nuns we have the following way to handle our difficult emotions without expecting our partners or friends to contain them for us. This is known as a "Compassion Exercise." It just takes a few minutes.

Close your eyes and breathe in 5 counts through your nose.
Breathe out 8 counts (seconds) through your lips.
Do this a few times until you feel relaxed.

Focus on your unpleasant feeling and breathe it in slowly. Maybe it's despair.

1. Imagine your lungs purifying the despair and turning it into golden light which you then exhale. This is kind of like being a girl/boy scout where you take something and leave it cleaner than you found it. The energy around you is being lifted up, cleaned and purified.
Do this 3 times total.

2. Now take the same emotion for someone whom you love and repeat the inhale/exhale process for their despair. Do this 3 times total.

3. Now take the same emotion for someone whom you find difficult or think of as an enemy and repeat the inhale/exhale process for their despair.
Do this 3 times total.

4. Finally, take the same emotion for all the people in the world, all the countries and cultures, imagine them feeling this feeling (despair) and repeat the inhale/exhale process for their feeling.
Do this 3 times total.

UPSET AS OPPORTUNITY FOR GROWTH

This is a form for recording the details of upsetting events to reveal how your consciousness conflicts with reality. In other words, upset is your system's signal that old, inaccurate beliefs are being challenged by events. Recording these detailed events provides a chance to see patterns and clearly note when exactly the upset occurs.

1. Day, Date Time of upset:
2. Describe what was happening BEFORE you became upset. Who, what, When, Where, How?
3. Tell the facts of the upsetting event. And ONLY the facts.
4. When did you actually get upset? Find the TRIGGERING word or moment. The exact second you changed from ok to upset.
5. What feelings came up for you?
6. What were the exact words of the thoughts?
7. What actions did you take?
8. Can you identify a PART that came up?
9. Where do you feel it in your body?
10. Tell your PART: "It's ok to feel_______________."
11. Is the feeling familiar? When have you felt this before?
12. If you have time and/or desire sit with this PART and let her/him tell you more… everything.
13. If the PART is engaged in blaming, try turning it around: "He never considers my feelings!" To : " I never consider my feelings"…"I never consider HIS feelings".

5 STEPS FOR EMOTIONAL HYGIENE

Or

How to get access to your core SELF energy

1. **PART of me is feeling________________ (afraid, hurt, doubting, etc.)**

2. **It's OKAY to feel ______________________________ (Hurt, afraid, doubting, etc.)**

3. **It's MY WORK to look at this______________________________ (hurt, fear, shame, doubt, etc.)**
   No one can MAKE me feel anything, crawl in my skin and cause me to feel something.

4. **Where do I feel it in my BODY?**

5. **What do I want to do with it? Since emotions are energy, I can use this anger energy to journal, run, clean, scream, Fill out an "Upset as an Opportunity for Growth" form (see next page), exercise, beat a pillow, dance etc.**

ACRONYM: POW-Where-What.
An easy way to remember all 5 steps.

P = Part
O = Okay
W = Work
Where = in my body?
What = do I want to do?

5 STEPS FOR EMOTIONAL HYGIENE

Or

How to get access to your core SELF energy

1. PART of me is feeling ____________ (afraid, hurt, doubting, etc.)

2. It's OKAY to feel ____________________ (hurt, afraid, doubting, etc.)

3. It's MY WORK to look at this ____________________ (hurt, fear, shame, doubt, etc.)

   No one can MAKE me feel anything, crawl in my skin and cause me to feel something.

4. Where do I feel it in my BODY?

5. What do I want to do with it? Since emotions are energy, I can use this anger energy to journal, run, clean, scream, fill out an "Upset as an Opportunity for Growth" form (see next page), exercise, beat a pillow, dance, etc.

ACRONYM: POWW-Where-What

An easy way to remember all 5 steps.

P = Part

O = Okay

W = Work

Where = in my body?

What = do I want to do?

WATCHING

Putting a space of observation between what you are feeling and what you observe about your feelings is the key to operating from a central calm core instead of a person going to pieces. This is the principle behind psychotherapy, where just talking about what upset you seems to make it less awful the next time it happens.

What I propose is not original, but maybe I can state it in a way that helps you. There is a central, calm core to who you are. Nothing you can do will destroy it…even the worst trauma! According to Richard Schwartz, the originator of IFS (internal Family Systems) work, this core is always available to be tapped into. Your core is calm, wise, clear, confident, compassionate and many other of your highest qualities. It is an Observer Self.

The more your watch your feelings, the more you engage this core. And by the way, the watching enhances your feeling alive and engaged because you are fully present in the moment.

TESHUVAH OR THE RETURN TO WHOLENESS

Shamans help people to health by retrieving soul fragments that get lost at certain traumatic times of the victims' lives. In ancient Jewish mysticism called "Kabbalah" the same idea is also held that there is a basic health that gets broken or disrupted with trauma. In Energy Healing, any stuck traumas or frozen negative emotions cause a disruption in our energy flow and health: physical, mental or emotional. In studying Jewish mysticism for 15 years I learned the following steps to help us move on when it's almost impossible to forgive. This is really important in relationships; there's the principle of the wholeness that follows forgiveness combined with an energy healing tool of meditative visualization.

The 5 Steps of Forgiveness Also called the Return to the Divine Within or Teshuvah.

Imagine yourself and the person who has wronged you.

Picture a circle of supportive people around you—not everyone—just the ones who make you feel really loved and comfortable. They are the witnesses.

Imagine yourself telling the story of the rape, the betrayal, the theft, the murder, etc., whatever you have found impossible to forgive. See your circle of supportive, loving people listening to you and acknowledging what happened.

Now it's time for you to imagine the perpetrator speaking these 5 steps:

1. I admit wrongdoing
2. I feel remorse
3. I promise never to do this again (the person may be dead, but the golden light of her/ his soul can do this. It's very important so the ongoing trauma can be lifted from you! Otherwise you continue to be punished and blocked for what they did to wrong you.)
4. I am sorry!
5. What can I do to make it up to you, if anything? This can be imagined and still has a positive effect on your subconscious.

Give thanks for this healing.....

RESCUE TRIANGLE

This is a symbol devised by Stephen Karpman. It represents how relationships become unstable when one person feels she/he must rescue another. Rescuing is based on the false idea that we are not all equal in our responsibility to direct our own lives and choices. That we must step in and do for others, who are not capable to taking on their own responsibility.

Sally does her teenage kids' laundry. They are fully capable of doing it themselves, but have never been asked to because Sally feels sorry for them with their high school workloads. She sees them as powerless Victims. Both her twins leave dirty clothes on the floor of their bedrooms. Sometimes Sally feels out-of-control angry while picking up the clothes, and finds herself yelling at them. When that happens, Sally has flipped position from the Rescuer to Persecutor.

The Rescuer often becomes tired and resentful from giving out so much energy. He/she may even get angry and become the Persecutor of the victim. (By getting angry and yelling)

The person being rescued eventually must switch positions because it is not healthy to remain in the powerless victim position. In the case of Sally, the twins hate listening to her outbursts and may rudely yell back, taking on the role of the Persecutor. They could also break out of the Rescue Triangle by doing their own laundry. This would make the family run more functionally and feel better to everyone.

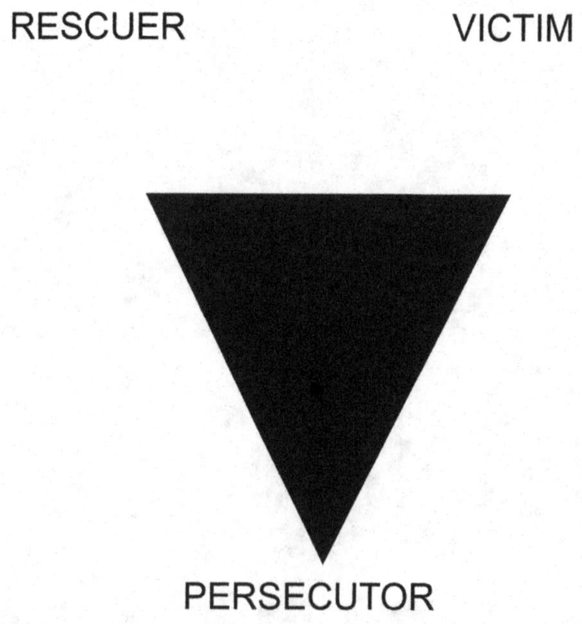

As you can see, the Rescue Triangle is unstable and can flip at any time. When people see themselves as Victims or Rescuers, anger and retaliation are sure to follow. When there's anger in your relationship, look for a Rescue Triangle as a possible cause!

ANGER

Do not be afraid of anger.

It's a natural and powerful part of our existence.

It lets us change things that we don't like or need.

It energizes us if we let it flow.

Cats do it!

Dogs do it!

Even Baboons do it!

Annoyance, anger, hostility— Watch them come, watch them go.

You are not your thoughts. You are not your feelings. There is a central divine core to you that is wise, clear and calm.

An average emotion lasts 90 seconds if you don't hold onto it. The temporary flow of anger keeps a relationship from getting stuck or boring or stale.

All couples have conflict at times. Allow negative feelings to teach us more about the reality of our present and or just let them pass...However, if your relationship includes abuse, violence and/or constant anger and negativity, see a counselor. Make sure to keep yourself safe and face the message that it's time to go.

A LAST WORD

Each relationship has its own unique course. This book, as you may have guessed, touches the tip of the iceberg in what it means to participate in a loving, intimate and satisfying relationship. Relationships are mysterious and very much like journeys. They keep changing, and seem to have cycles of difficulty and ease. They teach us all the time if we are awake and open to learning. To encourage that learning is the goal of this book.

The contents here are a guide to create “safety” — a spacious, harmonious and protected environment where each person can really be him/herself. Building love with others is the key to our utilizing the incredible individual assets of our authentic selves.

Remember: You are not your thoughts.

You are not your feelings.

There is a core of you that is way beyond either of these!